HAPPINESS REINVENTED

Igniting Principles of Being the Best You can Be

Dr. Suresh Devnani

"You are a living magnet: You attract into your life people, situations, and circumstances that are in harmony with your dominant thoughts."

— Dr. Suresh Devnani

The Must Have Guide

Copyright © 2014 Dr. Suresh Devnani.

All Rights Reserved.

Reproduction or translation of any part of this work beyond that permitted by Section 107 or 108 of the 1976 United States Copyright Act without the permission of the copyright owner is unlawful. Request for permission or further information should be addressed to the Permissions Department, Dr. Devnani & Associates.

The people and events described and depicted in this novel are fictitious and any resemblance to actual incidents or individuals is unintended and coincidental.

No part of this book may be reproduced, stored in a retrieval system or transmitted in any form by an electronic, mechanical, photocopying, recording means or otherwise without prior written permission of the publisher.

ISBN: 978-981-07-8143-9

This Book is dedicated to:

My ever supportive Father, Mother, Wife and amazing Children

Table of Contents

Why Should I Read This Book? 11
    Are you Pessimist or Optimist? 17

Why Am I Writing This Book? 25

1: YOUR RIGHT TO BE 27
    Mindset of Winner 29
    3 Common Kinds of Mindsets 31
    So What is Determination? 34
    What is Discipline? 35

2: YOUR MIND AN ELECTRO MAGNET 39
    Focusing On Our Thoughts Can Increase
    The Magnetism 41
    Mindful Magnetism 44

3: THE RESTLESS MIND 47
    The Following Are The Signs Of A Restless Mind 48

4: DOING WHAT YOU LOVE 55

5: PURSUIT OF HAPPINESS 61
    So what is True Happiness? 62

    There are two Approaches to True Happiness 64

    So How Do You Find True Happiness? 67

6: BEING EMPATHETIC 67
    Effective Communication 68

    Robust Imagination 68

    Where does empathy come from? 71

7: FEAR OF LOSING LOVED ONES 75
    The seven emotional stages of Grief 77

    Simple Ways to Help Someone Who's Grieving 77

    Listen 77

    Never Rush An Emotional Moment 78

    Speak About The Person That Passed Away 78

    Be Honest Over Clichés 78

    Compassion 78

8: DECISION MAKING FOR WINNERS 81

    Develop Your View 82

    Establish The Right Conduct 82

    Train Your Mind 83

    Focus On Happiness 83

    Stay Interconnected 83

    Stay Positive 84

9: OUR ATTITUDE REFLECTS OUR LIFE 87

    The Blueprint to Positive Personal Development 90

10: AWAKENING AND LOVING YOUR 95

    Are You Truly Happy Being So Engaged? 96

EPILOGUE 101

    Where Do You Go From Here? 102

Why Should I Read This Book?

You may have just picked this book up, or you may have just bought it, or it may have been given to you. And from the look on the cover, it appears to be just another 'self-help' book. But before you completely reject the possibility of reading it, thinking that like the rest, it proposes yet another mystical principle of the Universe, appropriating misunderstood and unrelated Laws of Physics to self help and claiming to be able to make you rich beyond your wildest dreams, give it one more page.

Improving your life or 'Happiness Reinvented' as this book suggests is not all about getting rich nor is it about being the healthiest man alive. I know that as I say this, some of you are already shaking your heads in disapproval, insolently insisting: "Yes it is!". And I honestly do agree to some extent that I would rather cry and pity myself in my Mercedes over the back seat of a public city bus. But the key to 'Happiness' is not about the number of digits on the end of your bank statement, or the number of cars you have, or the proximity of your house from the 'oh so important city center', at the end of the day, it is all really about being in the winning mindset.

As I write this, I can't help but wonder how many of you scoffed at that last line or remarked 'Way to go Sherlock! I didn't need to buy this book to hear that!' Your thoughts may have then drifted to something along the lines of: 'I can never be truly happy because, well... people are starving all over the world, there are bombings and acts of terror everywhere, and I have to constant burden to work to put food on the table.' If you aren't thinking these things and are honestly convinced that you are truly happy or never want to be, then it is time to shut this book and move on with your life, because the reality is that I probably cannot help you.

If you've gotten this far, then I believe 'congratulations' are in order. Because the first step in order to become truly happy, is *wanting* to be. I know of so many people, including myself at one point who would rather remain unhappy and fill themselves with self-pity then choose to be happy. In a way, this is everyone at one point in our lives, but if you have chosen to take control of your life and make an active effort to improve it, then I commend you, because the first step is changing your attitude.

But despite the fact that you have made it this far, you may still linger in doubt as to how helpful this book is going to be. I mean, go to the bookstore and check out the self-help section, and ask yourself: 'How many of these books promise to make me rich, healthy, content, popular or loved? How many of them will keep that promise? On top of this, there may be thoughts going through your mind along the lines of: "What will my friends think if I start following a book with the hope it will one day make me truly happy. What will my spouse think? What will parents think?" And to be completely honest, if I were in your place, I would never believe that a book, a book that weighs less than a kilogram, that I may have come across by random chance is going to change my life. In fact, in the modern world, it may be seen as naive to think so.

I know 'happiness' may sound like a far-fetched idea that many other books have promised to give you, but the reason they aren't able to do so is because they outline impractical methods of magical formulas that never seem to work. And it's tempting to believe they do, because for all we know, maybe they do and we just aren't applying the methods correctly. But the sad truth is that in life, there is no 'quick fixes' to major problems. But what I can tell you is that if you read this book, I will show you real and practical ways to be human, and still be happy, with methods reaping real and practical results. These methods are those that I have personally tested to make me content. And I am not talking about an excerpt from that one so called 'success story' from the hundreds that have tried my methods, but I am referring to results you will see in yourself.

Because like you, I was fed up. I was absolutely fed up of walking into the bookstore on weekends, finding a book on happiness, finishing it by Monday, and still realizing that life was nothing more than a long wait for death. I began to ask myself whether I was falling or flying, whether I was living or dying? I know that reading a self-help book about business or finance for example, in which the author claims to teach you secret foolproof financial formulas to manipulating Wall Street aren't very reassuring when the author himself struggles to pay his rent. Some books claim to teach what the preacher cannot even master himself. But in this book all I ask is that you have a little faith, because I have been where you are now, I have been frustrated, melancholy, ashamed, bored, irritated, unhappy and to be honest, just fed up with life. I hope you appreciate the fact that I am not outlining a magical formula like the rest, and I am not asking you to connect to the mystical energy of the Universe to manifest your dreams. All I am asking you to do is to be human and to be yourself. There is no secret that only the greatest among us know – there is no genie in the lamp. There is, although, a mindset – a mindset that can improve your life. It does not come from scripture, but rather, it comes from science.

In just 2012 alone, the growth of scientific research in the field of Noetic Theory has gained greater attention and interest. Studies have been published studying the health effects of expecting good things to happen. A phenomenon that researchers call "dispositional optimism," and the vast majority of these research papers have examined the relationship between optimism and well-being. The results of these papers are shocking, showing that by having a positive outlook, individuals can enjoy reductions in their stress levels, improved health, enhanced relationship with family, friends, co-workers, a decrease in anxiety, anger, and their ability to manage physical pain more effectively, ultimately be happier.

When I first came across such papers, my skepticism got the better of me. Studies and experimentation that claim to investigate the effect of thoughts on the human body often contain too many uncontrolled variables, and are highly subjective in nature. Some of these experiments are just pseudoscience, funded by organizations with the ulterior motive of proving that God exists or that the Universe is alive. In addition, how can one ever claim to measure improvements in relationships and management of pain when both these figures are relative, and vary from person to person? But after reading a quote, I thought perhaps I would try a little experiment with myself. "Stop complaining for just 24 hours and see how your life begins to change". And so for 24 hours I instructed my family to tell me off any time I complained, and would start again. It took me nearly 6 months to go a whole day without complaining, and who knew we did it so many times without knowing? At first I must admit that the feeling was perturbing, I felt as if the negative thoughts of my dissatisfaction were building up inside my head and amassing my disapproval. But eventually, they subsided, and for the first time in a long time, they failed to return. All of a sudden I didn't have anything bad to say about people, things or situations. Not only did I appreciate the people and things around me more, but I also had a whole new level of insight into situations that was foreign to me. Rather than looking at my problems as obstacles, I saw them as opportunities. This paradigm shift in perception only required a day without complaining, and all of a sudden, I had clarity on a whole new level. This was a mindset, a mindset that translated itself into the physical world. Not only did I come up with new business opportunities that I had never before even remotely considered, but I also enjoyed a better relationship with my family and friends, who simply appreciate a positive and more upbringing attitude over any other.

From these scientific studies, we now know the reasons why optimists are more successful than pessimists, and the secret lies in the way in which they manage, perceive and therefore handle things in life. Optimists have enhanced skills in problem solving; they stay focused and take every opportunity in improving the situation. Physically, they take better care of their health, they maintain a proper diet, exercise, and sleep well.

Pessimists, on the other hand, do the opposite they keep denying, avoiding, and deform the problems they tackle, and are settled on their negative feelings. But most of all, pessimists enter a deadly spiraling cycle that leads them away from their ambitions, down a dangerous road to depression and failure.

Are you now thinking that this is just another book promising to turn you from a pessimist into an optimist? Or are you abandoning the first question all-together because you think you're already an optimist? Your likely answer to both those questions is a Yes, but do you want to know the harsh truth? Chances are you are not yet an optimist or at least, not one most of the time, and to be honest with you it's not your fault. Situations around us can be put together in such perfect coordination that being irritated, annoyed or burned out is inevitable. It may sometimes feel that a divine or supernatural force is out there to make your life a living nightmare. This can frequently lower our expectations for the future, expecting nothing more than the terrible day you may think you are having today. But the reality is that it doesn't have to be this way.

Being a pessimist is passive, being an optimist takes effort. And if your are happy being miserable all the time, then its time to put this book back down or give it away, because it isn't written for you.

Are you Pessimist or Optimist?

Think about some awkward events that have taken place in your life, and try to remember how you proceeded in managing those situations.

It is no doubt that our thoughts influence our behavior, attitude, our life, and all those people surrounding us. Our thoughts are like a video we play. Whatever video we play, is what we see and think. Thoughts that we keep repeating influence our over well being.

If you don't believe me, lets try a little experiment. Tonight before going to bed, think about a single idea. It may be the girl of your dreams (hopefully this is your wife if your married), images of luxury, a place, or a time you remember. Chances are, if you successfully do this for a number of nights, that on one of those nights, this idea will appear in your dreams. When this occurs, it has entered your subconscious mind. Wondering why you keep having nightmares? Perhaps its time to cut down on the amount you watch the news, dramatized shows and horrific video games. My son used to have a chronic problem with nightmares as a child, which came to a point where he became scared to go to sleep. And the cure: stop watching Scooby Doo, scary movies and ghost hunting shows. And his problem was cured. It was the stimulus around him that was affecting his subconscious mind.

This does not mean in order to be happy you must isolate yourself from the world, shave your head, live in a cave and meditate all day long. All that is required is for you to strike a balance between how much you preoccupy yourself with matters that are negative in nature, and how much you appreciate circumstances that are positive in nature. The key here is to find an equilibrium. If you're a trader, this does not mean you should turn off CNBC or Bloomberg in the morning if they are providing you valuable information about your stock being a bad pick, but this means that you do not indulge in negativity more than you need to.

Therefore in order to make changes in our life, we need to make changes in our process of thinking. This is crucial if we want to see an improvement in our lives. If we think of our minds as a computer, it is no more complicated than deleting an old, outdated and pessimistic application, video or word document from our mind, and replacing it with a new and updated one. Think of it as upgrading to new software, your Life reinvented. By changing our mind-set in a way that will change our actions and attitudes, we will find ourselves being lead by people, situations and events that are similar to our thoughts.

This does not mean that by thinking positively, the Universe is going to respond and grant us with our hearts desires. It doesn't quite work that way, if it did, then our economy wouldn't seem to function. (Author Note: Can you imagine if we lived in a world where thinking of a Ferrari hard enough made it spontaneously appear, I would probably be more busy driving my endless garage of new cars instead of writing this book.) But what thinking positively can do is change the way in which we look at the world. It's all about this single idea of perception. A successful man does not live in a different world from the financially troubled one; he wasn't given opportunities that weren't available to others around him. But what made him happy is the way in which he perceived those opportunities and solved problems.

A single thought is not strong enough to make any significant change, but if we keep repeating that thought, this allows momentum to be built. (Author Note: I am not quoting any concept of Physics such as Momentum or the Law of Gravitational Attraction, and vaguely relating it to the ideas of this book. There is no need for false connections and pseudoscience in what I am trying to teach you, the ideas in this book do not need scientific backing of a false nature. If you wish to seek proof, then all you must do is willingly try). Focusing and repeating on our thoughts allows our subconscious mind to change our lives and how we perceive our environment. The best part of this technique is we don't even need to overexert or strain ourselves for it to transpire. All it requires is that we select a thought that we wish would come true, and keep repeating it.

Presume that you are afraid of heights, and you would like to change this condition. By forcing yourself to stand on ledge of a building will not work, and make you feel more miserable and scared. Wouldn't it be easier if you were to visualize standing on the highest viewing deck of the Eiffel Tower, feeling secure and safe? By repeating this you will be developing an ideal mind set to accomplish whatever you want. Visualization is a powerful and easy technique that has been scientifically proven to help individuals. Australian Psychologist Alan Richardson decided to test the effectiveness of Visualization techniques with a number of basketball players. The participants were divided into 3 groups in which one group was asked to practice for 20 minutes each day, while the other was asked to visualize themselves making free throws, but no real practice was allowed. The third group was a control, not allowed to practice or visualize. The results were astounding, which showed that there was a significant improvement in the group that just visualized, who were almost as proficient as the group that practiced, and preformed much better than the control group who weren't allowed to visualize or practice at all.[1]

On a similar note, for those of you who have children, this idea is also applicable. Consider your response to your child when he or she returns home with a poor school report card or bad grades. Chances are you express your disappointment in your child, while many parents go even further as to condemn their performance and remind them that they are on their way to failure. This is a destructive cycle, and it teaches the most impressionable members of our society, our children, that they cannot succeed, that they were born failures, and fill them with fear. If you find yourself in this situation, perhaps you may consider trying out a new method. If your child brings home poor grades, sit them down and explain to them the consequence of their actions in an optimistic tone. Remind them that they can reach for the stars if they just tried. And like in most cases, you will see that your child's self- realization and visualization of their dreams will take them far further than criticism or fear ever will.

By focusing our thoughts with definite details, color, sound, smell, and mentally being part of this picture and follow through with determined resolve, the subconscious mind will start accepting this as truth, allowing the necessary changes to take place for it to become a reality.

Your thoughts will overcome habits and build encouraging habits, acquire new skills and abilities, and begin to change your conditions and realize anything that you truly desire. The control over your thoughts can help in starting a new business, improve your relationships, have more money, happiness, calm and improvement of overall well being.

All this will not materialize overnight. It takes time, honesty in your efforts and how inclined you are with this new way of thinking.

This is psychological training that requires support from all three elements: your mind, heart and body. We must maintain an accessible mind and be ready to take action whenever this moment appears in our sight.

Firstly we must have a clear picture of what we want to achieve or become, and stay determined and inclined with our thoughts repeating this process at pre-set times during the day for it to become into reality. Repeating these thoughts will build a momentum, allowing for both inner and outer changes in you. Supremacy over your thoughts is the key in transforming, improving and mastering your life.

If you find yourself becoming skeptical at this point, wondering how this may happen and how your reality may change, you must always remember that your reality is relative; relative to the way you view and process it. In the study of philosophy, this is known as relativism, and proposes that any perspective only has varying degrees of truth and validity. If we reconsider this idea within the context's of our disposition on life, we may realize that the way we view the world is not absolute, but constantly changes. If you don't agree, try this little thought experiment:

Think back to your childhood, and put yourself back into the shoes of 5-year-old you. Did the world seem so bad then? Now put yourself the shoes of 15 or 16 year old you, and consider how the world seemed to you then. Now bring yourself back to the present. Chances are your personality, ambitions, dreams and desires all changed throughout the course of your life. You may blame this on changing times, increased terrorism, new political ideologies, the loss of a loved one, but fundamentally, the world out there is more or less the same. From when you were young, to what it is now. The world didn't change your disposition; instead your disposition changed the world (at least in your eyes).

There is no right or wrong, secrets or mysteries about superior growth. I did not find the secret to happiness inscribed on a scroll in a glass bottle at sea one day. But rather, in this book I am simply revealing time-tested results. Mind-enriching, and purposeful actions are essential in order to ascertain order in our lives and provide us opportunity for authentic transcendent growth. Purposeful living results in success and creates purpose of being.

It is possible that you have read others books, listened to CD's, watched DVD's and or attended numerous get rich courses on business, real estate, or stocks. Why then have you not reached your full potential? The reason may be because some of these courses offer impractical solutions to success. The main reason may be something from within yourself, usually childhood influences that act as self-defeating thoughts, which are not letting your future connect to the abundance of love, joy, harmony, peace, health, vitality and wealth. Besides this, most of you are looking in the wrong direction.

Throughout this book, we will explore what abundance is at its core, how to prepare yourself in receiving more of all good things, and how you can transform any limiting beliefs that you have held up until now.

On a final note, it is a proven fact of psychology that we are more likely accept what we wish to believe, and often forget to ask ourselves; 'What are the facts?'.

"When you are studying any matter, or considering any philosophy, ask yourself only: What are the facts, and what is the truth that the facts bear out. Never let yourself be diverted, either by what you wish to believe, or what you think could have beneficent social effects if it were believed; but look only and solely at what are the facts."

Bertrand Russell, Philosopher,

Dr. Suresh Devnani

Nobel Laureate

This book is not a compilation of mysterious kitchen-like recipes that will allow you to master the mysterious spells and unending powers of the Universe. In fact, this book is nothing of the sort, and has no affiliation with such delusion. This book is veritable self-help, the act of helping yourself through practical and proven methods, not the promise of a secret formula. You cannot wish your way to success, and as demoralizing as that sounds, that does not mean reaching success is impossible. But rather, it can make the journey all the more attractive and glorious. And if you find yourself on a low note in life at the moment, always remember that no matter who you are, no matter where you come from, no matter what color, race, language, or religion, you have every right, and the same potential to be successful and happy, but the first step is wanting to be.

"Only if you have been in the deepest valley, can you ever know how magnificent it is to be on the highest mountain."

Richard Nixon,

37th President of the United States

Why Am I Writing This Book?

It was Friday afternoon in early 2000 and I had just returned from a late lunch with my private banker who was asking me to clear my outstanding dues. My employees had left for the day and I was alone in the office. Business was dropping steadily for some time, and I had just found out from my financial planner that I had lost my savings in a speculative investment I had made earlier in the year. Everything was falling apart. I was seriously depressed, considering suicide, as I was facing some of the most serious problems of my life. I was thinking that if I ended my life now, then my family could use my life insurance policy of $5 million dollars as a new beginning. Like all of you, I loved my family, and was willing to do whatever it takes for them to be happy.

Life had seemed like a tunnel with no end. All I kept asking is why me? Why does this have to happen to me? I'm just trying to take care of my wife, my son. I'm not trying to beg, rob or steal. I just want to live and be happy. Why does that have to be impossible?

Focusing all my attention on negative thoughts, I allowed failure, and mental torture to enter my life. Finally I had the courage to tell my family of the problems that I was facing, as I saw no light at the end of the tunnel. My wife and my 5 year old son said don't worry we can simplify our life, removing all the unnecessary expenses, and making new start. With their support and new awakening, I started to look at my core beliefs and realized that even though I was saying that I wanted to be rich and happy, I had lost the secret of being happy.

Like most people in difficult times, I started to ask questions like; Why did I fail? What did I do wrong? Why me? As I looked for answers for the above questions, my thoughts were full of negative feelings towards others and especially myself.

Our thoughts and feelings are like a powerful magnet, which can attract or prevent success. They don't get the Universe to manifest what we think of, but our thoughts and mindset can make us miss opportunities, and focus on the problems rather than the solutions. We need to mold our beliefs and expectations about failure or success.

I hope this book will inspire, motivate and help you to improve your life and help you gain all the success you desire. **Because you deserve it.**

"If I repeat a thought long enough, surely I will become that way."

— Mahatma Gandhi

1

YOUR RIGHT TO BE

A WINNER

If you look around you, you will see that people who regularly win have winning thoughts. Winning is a state of Mind, and we all can be winners if we start thinking and making decisions like a winner.

The first thing you have to realize before you go any further is that winning is not a destiny, it is a choice. Happiness is not for the lucky, or the blessed, or the chosen ones among us, but rather, Happiness is a property that exists in all men and women alike, colored or white, Asian or American, tall or short, rich and poor. And one of the greatest problem that so many people I train experience, is that they honestly believe that according to their Palmistry, to a, Astrological Chart, Numerology or a Fortune Teller, that they are destined to fail and be miserable, to be limited by divine forces they cannot control. They believe, that some God or Deity that wishes for them to be poor and suffer loss has predetermined their life. These are not winners - these are people who let pseudoscience take control of their lives. These are people who let others define how far they can go. These are people who will never grow, because they never realize until they day after they die, that greatness was within them.

Most people are restricted by their negative thoughts that prevent them from fully utilizing all the resources available to them. While many individuals may disagree with this statement, it is not difficult to observe this in our everyday lives.

Most negative thoughts come from two sources: First being conditioning which has been passed on to us by our parent's, relatives, teachers, community and friends who have told us what we can and can't do and your mind has taken all this to be true for everything you do.

The second source of negative thoughts comes directly from your very own brain's defense mechanisms. Your thinking and physiological systems are all working to protect you from harm that have been conditioned by our first source. This defense mechanism is actually working on pre-conditions set by our early growth which is self limiting our potential to be a winner.

You are now an adult and have a very capable mind to help you make your very own judgment.

Your journey to winning begins with "winning thoughts".

These are inspirations that push your spirit high, when your imagination takes wings and you dream about achieving great things beyond your comprehension.

A winner is a person who has determination, who is disciplined, who is motivated, has the desire in improving his life, willing to acquire new skills, willing to overcome obstacles and challenges, and wants to rise to the top in his field of expertise.

Mindset of Winner

- Has a 'can do' attitude.
- Passionate, loves what they do.
- Grateful for all they have.
- Helps others to succeed. Does not envy everyone else.
- Self-Confidence, believes in their self.
- Forgiving Heart, forgives others easily.

There is no doubt that most of us admire, envy, and respect winners, who have the great power of succeeding in whatever they do.

There are several reasons why we should never be envious of another person's success that denotes one never being satisfied with anything one ever achieves.

By being envious of other people's success, we are essentially informing ourselves that we do not know what we want from our own lives. Just because John Doe has this or does that, does not mean that you need the same. Wouldn't it better that you set your own objectives? By having a clear vision for your own life, what another person achieves or acquires won't matter: you will know exactly where you are, why you are there, where you need to go and what you need to do to get there, you can Win.

Wouldn't it be better that you channel all your energy into your own success by thinking of ways in improving your own situation? It may often be tempting to expend our energy in criticizing others, finding their flaws and making ourselves feel marginally more confident about ourselves. But in the long term, criticizing does no good. More often than not, the very individuals who you criticized may have been hurt initially, but then may have received your thoughts in a more constructive nature, thereby improving themselves. Think about this, and you'll realize it's true. Your efforts in bringing someone down always backfire, and will only send them higher. Criticism is not a bad thing, and it should never be used as a weapon. If you need to criticize, channel that into yourself and make yourself the best you can be.

My son was someone who was a very timid public speaker in his early years, and was heavily criticized for it, being told that he would always do better on the sidelines and away from the limelight. Initially, I could tell it hurt him, and in reality it can diminish your spirit and self esteem, especially in a child. But in the long run, it drove him to push harder, and by the age of sixteen was awarded the Top National Award for Debate and Public Speaking in Singapore. And the one thing he told me that night years ago was: 'What if I had accepted their view of me? What if I had accepted myself as a timid speaker? Surrendered to a life that was nothing like what I dreamed of?' That is precisely the point, not only did that criticism hurt him, but sent him higher. But more than that, despite how hard it is, despite how deep and sheltered that faucet of greatness is within you, we have to find it. We have to search, even if it takes months, years, or a lifetime. But what only few in life can tell you, is that it exists within every man.

3 Common Kinds of Mindsets

Win/Lose: Are those that compare themselves to other people all the time. They believe that in order for them to succeed others must fail.

Lose/Lose: Are those that believe they can never achieve anything worthwhile so why should they let you do so. They will only criticize, and are negative about anything and everything.

Win/Win: They believe that their success depends on other people's success.

If you want to succeed in life and become the person you are meant to be, then you must know that you will not get there alone. Therefore you must help others to succeed and to become great if you are to be great yourself. It is often said that the greatest people are always those that help others.

Learn to be happy about others' success and look forward to your own success. Do not judge yourself based on what others have achieved, but rather based on what you want to achieve. Compete with yourself. Depending on what you want in life, their success could be failure to you or vice versa, but it should not matter to you either way.

Life is not a one-man race or a race against other people. There is no finish line, no goal, and no objectives. You determine the destination, the route, the time limits and the prize. We are all running a different race. How do you compete with someone that is not on the same track as you are?

Never be envious or jealous of others, as this is adverse habit that will only steal your energy, creativity, drive, and clarity of mind.

Don't use money as a gauge of your success – it is an instrument to be happy, not a yardstick. In my training seminars, I have met countless individuals who were not ashamed to proclaim with pride that they are a cashier at Wal-Mart, or that they worked in the mailroom under some of America's Largest Banks. But unlike so many executives and professionals that go to work each day dreading the task before them, they go to work with integrity and pride. They are the unsung heroes of our society because without them, the world would fail to work. Lawyers are classified as some of America's top earners, but why are they some of America's unhappiest people? Money does not buy happiness, but the character and mindset that you build does.

Happiness Reinvented

If your dreams are your fire, then your "winning words" are your fuel. In our daily lives we all indulge in talking to ourselves. There is that voice within us that says - "I can do this", or "this is not so tough", or "hang on, this too shall pass". Winning is about making these inner voices your "real voice". It is about bringing the winning thoughts out in open and making them "winning words". It is about taking them out from the world of dreams and imagination into the real world where they can be heard; by you and others.

The fact is that being a Winner is a trainable skill and everyone can acquire more determination, discipline, and motivation through practical techniques.

Determination and discipline are the key elements that can help in your inner game, as they are crucial tools for success in all avenues of your life. They can easily be trained and acquired like any other skill, yet only few take the opportunity. This game changing skill is not reserved for the special ones, it is there for everyone to acquire and take advantage of.

I understand that adopting this mindset can be difficult, and ridding yourself of envy, jealousy and a desire for power sound nearly impossible. But in my experience, it is not so much as to being the perfect human being that makes us happy, but more, the trying to be a better person that gives us a sense of purpose. For many of the individuals I have trained, I have realized that it is the lack of a purpose, or a specific way of life that has brought about this emptiness within them. While I cannot say that any given way of life is better than another, I have seen hundreds of people find closure by attempting to live more simply.

An example of a philosophy that I have seen many individuals adopt is that of the Desiderata, A Poem of a Way of Life by Max Ehrmann. For copyright reasons, I cannot publish it in this book, but just like the Desiderata, I strongly recommend you look for a simple philosophy from which you can guide your life. Whether it be religious, spiritual or new age, as long as it feels right to you, it cannot be wrong.

So What is Determination?

Determination is the inner game, and one of the greatest assets one-can posses. Determination helps in making specific decisions, actions, behavior, execution of anything we aspire until it is accomplished, and regardless of any form of resistance, discomfort or difficulties which one faces during the process and further it always brings out the best in us.

Determination is the device one applies to defeat discouragement. Determination is the instrument one utilizes to overcome momentary failure to prevent failure from becoming everlasting. Determination is the apparatus one can apply to produce patience. Determination is the trick one practice to feed ones faith and starve ones fears about death.

Determination is the greatest character builder. It aide's one in meeting all ones commitments. It assists one to prioritize and manage ones time to maximize positive outcomes.

Determination is the ultimate technique one applies to win.

Determination is the device one uses to help win in spite of our limitations and dig oneself out of a hole.

Determination is the gadget that one can practice to improve ones relationships. Determination is the instrument one exploits to reach ones goals. Determination in simple words is the strategy one uses to succeed in all one wants to achieve.

Determined people are active, positive thinkers, and are willing to take the challenge upon them even in unpleasant or unknown circumstances.

What is Discipline?

Discipline is the ability to stick to our actions, thoughts and behaviors that guide us to improvement and success. Discipline comes with self-control, and requires our mental, emotional and physical attention.

Disciplined people don't require instant gratification, as they are always looking towards something better.

I am not saying that discipline requires living a life full of limitations or restrictions, in fact I am suggesting the opposite, as we want to acquire the ability of focusing all our energy and resolve towards accomplishment of our objective.

Both determination and discipline are needed for all our actions and decisions in order to maximize our success for all our endeavors from simple to complex tasks.

Whether you are a CEO of a Fortune 500 company or a

Dr. Suresh Devnani

Medical Intern at the bottom of the ladder, the key to success is about having the mindset of a winner. Our thoughts dictate our moods, which dictate our emotions, which dictate our body language and, ultimately, determine our ability to perform. Ensuring the way you approach a challenge mentally is correct is the key to success.

Winning thoughts are easy to think. Winning words are easy to say. But the key to it all is action! This requires energy, enthusiasm, commitment and taking responsibility to make your dreams real. But the reason why so many people never actually win is that they are not prepared to do what it takes to win. This is surprising as most people already know what it will take to win - they just don't take the action towards it! And knowing how to win but not doing it produces the same result as not knowing how to win!

Talk is cheap. The next big step is turning our winning words into winning actions. And if you have a good idea, stop talking about it. Because if it truly is a good idea, telling it to your friends and colleagues will result them implementing it before you do. Talking will get you nowhere, be proactive – implement your dreams and work towards them. Stop lying there on your bed waiting for money to fall out of the sky because you're manifesting it using your mind. It just doesn't work that way. If you're scared, remember: you came into this world with nothing, and you're going to leave this world with nothing. What's the worst that could possibly happen, and how can you loose something when you never had it to start off with? We're all going to die, so why not take risks? If you win, you will be happy; if you loose, you will be wise.

Happiness Reinvented

Nothing ventured, nothing gained.

Personal Development is a powerful weapon to counteract the numerous negative thoughts that plagues us. Napoleon Hill writes in the book, Think and Grow Rich, "that if you can conceive it you can achieve it." Your goals had to be bigger than the negative thoughts spinning in your head.

The world's top winners have a strong connection with their inner thoughts and they regularly train these thoughts like an Olympic athlete would train their body, to make it work in their favor.

"All action results from thought, so it is thoughts that matter."

— Sai Baba

2

YOUR MIND AN ELECTRO MAGNET

Your mind is composed of the thoughts you think. These thoughts are like magnetic streams. Thoughts themselves are a very specific form of consciousness energy, and all thoughts and permutations of thought exist in this non-local place. When you think thoughts and continue to think the same thoughts, you connect and bind to thoughts of the same type. This then binds with more thoughts and the cycle continues. Eventually, the thought becomes so powerful that it is able to influence physical situations and circumstances directly.

The influence in fact, it does not just attract our own thoughts but all similar thoughts from many sources, including other people. This is not a conscious act any more than an actual magnet consciously attracts.

There are several ways to supercharge your mind and thoughts with magnetic power. Strong desire, concentration and belief are some of the significant ingredients for infusing power into your thoughts.

Many activate the magnetic power of their mind unconsciously, without knowing what they are doing. When you know the rules, you become able to activate the magnetic power of your mind consciously, positively and effectively.

Visualizing and thinking with concentration, desire and faith, and repeating these thoughts often, releases powerful energy. Your thoughts get radiated and broadcasted, influencing the minds of other people, and attracting to you people who think along the same lines as you do and who can help you with your plans. This process also heightens your awareness ad perceptiveness of any opportunity connected with your thoughts that comes your way, and fills you with the inner power and initiative to utilize it.

A lot of research is being done in this area, and the developments are exciting. The field of Noetic Sciences is producing genuine physical evidence as to the effects of this phenomenon.

Our mind can be directed to any thought we choose with enough mental effort, and that results in creating what has been referred to as a magnetic center.

Any thought, positive or negative, if concentrated on long enough builds into a spiritualized material magnet that draws to the person those things that are in harmony with that thought. Therefore the Power of Thought to create anything you desire.

Focusing On Our Thoughts Can Increase The Magnetism

There are numerous ways to increase the power of your thoughts, and one of those ways is focusing. By increasing your focus, you are able to rationalize your thoughts and only be able to think in a certain way. Focusing is a vital tool to magnetize your thoughts and harness more thought power. By harnessing more power and expanding the power of thought, you will be able to harness more influence over the physical environment around you.

This is in fact is one of the greatest secrets of this century that only a few understand or have appreciated. The secret here is that your thoughts can be increased in strength through the power of your mental focus. Henry Ford discovered this secret and was able to create a $100 billion dollar business, becoming one of the richest men in the United States. In fact he himself had no formal education and was living a simple lifestyle until he was able to use the power of this resource to his full advantage.

Besides him other great minds, like Andrew Carnegie and Thomas Edison also discovered this secret.

The Law of Attraction and many other programs that are available today have grown out of a book called Think and Grow Rich by Napoleon Hill written shortly after the great depression in 1930. Napoleon Hill explains that the thought has a varying level of influence, depending on your mindset and behavior. The secret of how we think was given to him by Andrew Carnegie himself, who once used to be a bookkeeper working on a low wage, before becoming the richest man in America.

However, even Andrew Carnegie was not the originator of this method. The Kyballion, which is a study of the ancient Hermitic teachings dated 3,000 years ago, teaches these principles. A 21st century minded person does not easily absorb translated, mystical teachings.

The methods are quite clear:

1. Determine your goal
2. Make a plan
3. Be devoted to your goal
4. Finally, let it fill your mind

Indeed, this is all correct but it misses two important ingredients. The first is having contact with a living guide who has already succeeded in applying the techniques, a mentor in other words, and the second is the being part of support group, as Napoleon Hill suggested.

The problem with people is that we tend to lose track and motivation if we are on our own. The support group is the cure to that problem. It allows like-minded people to work through the techniques. Even if you are not all focused on your personal goal, you develop a connection through having a similar goal.

The techniques outlined of filling your mind with your dreams do not make them manifest themselves in mystical ways. But the charging of your mind as an electromagnet for success makes us makes decisions that take us there. Life is a journey of a thousand miles that can be broken down into many steps. And by filling our minds with thoughts of our dreams, what this does is make us walk in the right direction.

Lets say for example that your dream is to be healthier. If you fill your mind of positive thoughts of yourself with an amazing body, chances are the next time you eat out at your favorite restaurant, you'd be more inclined to skip dessert, because the process of filling your mind with your dream is making you walk in the right direction.

If your dream is to be affluent, then by filling your mind with thoughts of affluence and making a plan as outlined above, the chances are that the next time you're persuaded to purchase the latest mobile phone or designer bag, you'll be motivated to commit that money to your wealth management fund or investment, so that you can achieve your dream.

Notice that filling our minds with thoughts of our dreams does not manifest them into reality through mystical principles that we do not understand. But by filling our mind with the positivity of our aspirations, we essentially electro-charge our minds into motivating us to take us to where we need to go. It will diminish our fear, and empower our determination. As a result, we'll take realistic steps, stick to our plans, and constantly make decisions that make us walk on the right path in the right direction.

Leave the wishing to people who have accepted that they want to spend their lives hallucinating of their dreams. You are walking down a different path. You are walking towards your dreams. Because this method is not even remotely close to wishing. This is called being proactive. This is called the road to success.

Mindful Magnetism

Living in the present moment or commonly know as Mindfulness is being aware and conscious of your surroundings. From awareness, we evolve into the moment rather than regretting the past or fearing the future. It leads to full consciousness, even intuition.

As you commit your whole energy into the moment and you don't think about the future or the past. There is no past; all that exists is a series of records and your memory. All that exists is now. You only need to think about the things that you need to do in order to achieve your goals **and nothing else**. In this mindset, you are now able to advance at maximum speed towards your goal, as you are not being limited by the thoughts of the pre-conditioned past, or the desires of the future. You are simply investing your whole energy in the here and now, allowing you to achieve a maximum return in the here and now which can't be matched through any other means.

Through consistent and powerful efforts to strengthen the mind and allow it to operate at its most potent and powerful levels, the success you desire can be achieved in seemingly miraculous, unique and mysterious ways...all through the natural powers inherit within thought.

Improving your thought power will work a great deal to helping you achieve the success you want in life. To enhance the thought is about learning how to make your mind and body as efficient and as driven as possible.

"A ruffled mind makes a restless pillow."

— Charlotte Bronte

3

THE RESTLESS MIND

We all have restless minds mainly caused by our beliefs and past conditionings. We are so strongly engaged with our beliefs that it is tremendously difficult for us to understand that these are merely painful ideas and detaching from them can lead to peace and happiness. So many people have conditioned you that now you thoughtlessly believe your mind without even reflecting on the validity and understanding the effects this will have on your true state towards fulfillment and happiness. Our mind is set to manage external disturbances and upheavals that are continually going on within us both of these aspects interfere in our ability to focus and therefore are related to each other.

For example, if you are busy reading a book and suddenly there is a disturbance from someone watching television near the space were you are reading, you start focusing your thoughts associated with the person watching the television. The mind jumps from one thought to another. Despite of the fact that your eyes may be fixed on the book, the mind is actually far away and not registering what the eyes may be reading.

Another reason is stress, which is experienced by everyone and is an integral part of 21st century live. In school, work, or even at home, stress cannot be avoided. Stress can affect the daily activities in many ways than one. It can lead to poor motor functions and impede intellectual functions or how we think and behave. Stress can make you feel restless making it hard to focus and concentrate. Feeling restless can affect the quality of work of an individual. It leaves a feeling of uneasiness and discomfort.

The Following Are The Signs Of A Restless Mind

- **Impulsive:** You don›t have patience and you want it quick.

- **Anger:** You don›t tolerate the difference of opinion. You think that you are always right.

- **Depressed:** You get unhappy when there are some blocks in the fulfillment of your desires.

- **Disapproval:** You like it when others are seen to have faults.

- **Meddling:** You like poking your nose in others› business.

- **Arrogance:** You feel that you are the best and you like saying it also.

- **Lowliness:** You have low self-esteem and you tend to cringe in front of others.

- **Deferment:** You don›t like facing problems head on. You prefer postponing.

- **Fear:** You are scared of the future, or certain situations, or people.

- **Screaming:** You cannot tolerate people around you and you take them for granted.

- **Vengeance:** Even if you don›t say it, you like when somebody you don›t like gets hurt in some manner.

- **Hatred:** You cannot forgive. You don›t feel compassion for some people.

- **Frustration,** Lying, Adultery, Showing Off are some other signs showing that your mind is restless.

Resolving restlessness is a matter of focus and understanding. The simple rule to combat restlessness is to release our past and focus on the now. For most it may sound easy but harder to practice especially at the pinnacle of anxiety. Here are some techniques that will help manage restlessness through relaxation:

Deep breathing exercises: Practicing deep breathing can help calm the body and mind by increasing oxygen input and enhancing blood flow. Deep breathing expands the lungs by stretching its muscles and helps in maintaining optimum body functions.

Stretching: Has been found to help relieve muscle tensions and reduce the feeling of anxiety. This can also give the muscles a break from stress. It can be done in order to relieve the feeling of restless.

Rhythmic exercise: Rhythmic exercise can help improve blood circulation and relax the mind along with it. Rhythmic exercises include walking or jogging. These exercises do not put much stress on the muscles but can help improve breathing and calm the body.

Massage: A massage to the back or the whole body massage can help reduce stress and manage the feeling of restlessness in an individual. Massage improves blood flow and relaxes tense muscles.

New Age Programs: Like Tai Chi, Pilates, or yoga can help reduce stress and relieve restlessness. Each program has a specific method that can be followed in order to secure there full benefits. All of these programs have shown to improve circulation and reduce muscles tensions.

Water: Drinking water can help relax the nerves and reduce restless feeling as drinking water has shown to stimulate peristaltic movement and circulation to help relieve stress.

Sufficient Rest and Sleep: Rested body and mind helps in concentration and increase levels of energy.

Happiness Reinvented

Meditation: Meditation is a practice done by allowing the mind reach a state of focus and consciousness. Meditation can be done in a quite room with sufficient ventilation. Meditation can reap more benefits for the body aside from reducing the feeling of restlessness. Focusing on something that is not seen can help calm the mind and body. Although proper meditation can only be achieved through practice it can be done even if it is the first time a person meditates.

Do it for everyday for a couple of minutes to start with. Initially the mind will wander and you will not be able to concentrate. If you have the inclination and persist long enough, you will start enjoying the exercise and the mental peace that it provides. Gradually increase the time and go deeper to make contact with your inner self. As the inner self filters through, your emotions and the mind will slow down. That is the time you truly connect with yourself and realize the futility of irrelevant emotions.

Meditation is not a New Age phenomenon that will promise to reveal the meaning of life, but instead, it is an ancient technique to let the mind focus, and hones the mind to concentrate. Not only this, but in the relaxed character and mindset meditation helps to achieve, a new perspective of the world arises, and a new way of looking at things emerges. In this, you will see new innovative ideas, methods of solving your problems and a calm approach in dealing with them.

Hong Kong Business magnate Mr. Li Ka-Shing, Forbes 8th Richest Man in the World once said in an interview with a Hong Kong Broadcasting Network that business was like a game of golf. 'You may not tee off well, but if you keep calm, you can still save the hole'. This calmness is a state of mind that cannot be achieved overnight. But through practice of meditation and relaxation techniques, this new way in dealing with life can prove to be both beneficial and profitable in the long run.

Relaxation techniques have been developed in order to have the body and mind attain peace and comfort. Reaching the level of calmness and reducing stress and anxiety are the main goals of relaxation techniques. Any thing that can help improve blood circulation can help in relaxing.

There are instances that the restlessness is cause by medical conditions and can only be treated by addressing the health concern. It is best to seek the help of your health care provider during the times when restlessness in unmanageably or is already affecting your daily functioning. Pharmacological treatments and psychosocial treatments are also available to help relief the feeling.

The best way forward in regards to Meditation is to start in a simple and enjoyable manner. By meditating for short times between 5 to 15 minutes at a time. This will provide a beneficial foundation towards a stimulating mind frame.

Having our mind stay quiet, and on a fixed focus is one of your first challenges, therefore keeping things simple will be helpful.

I have found guided meditations to be a perfect start to help my mind to relax.

Happiness Reinvented

Guided meditations can help your mind get into the form required for more stimulating meditation. For those who prefer to meditate solo, please do go ahead, if you can allow your mind to stay quite and focused.

In starting with guided meditation, select the voice that you feel is the most soothing and you feel comfortable with, one that relaxes you and will help you to achieve the best results.

"If you do what you love, you'll never work a day in your life."

— Marc Anthony

4

DOING WHAT YOU LOVE

Money is a great driving force. But do what you love and the money will follow. But as any aspiring painter or starving musician can tell you, it just isn't that easy. Most people would say that finding a way to do what truly inspires and making money to support your desires can be a real challenge. Yet, from my own experience I say finding a way to follow your true calling is worth the effort and can allow life long results.

People who do what they love are happier, and are more productive, versus those who hate their jobs as suggested by experts.

Following are some reasons why it is important to do what one is passionate about.

Improved Self-Esteem: "Your self esteem will be higher because one feels energized by what they do, and your employer will be more prone to rewarding you for it,» As suggested by Sherry Mirshahi-Totten, a career advancement coach and the CEO and founder of Roadmap Career Services.

Self-Motivation: «Instead of being overwhelmed with stress for a job that you don›t even like, which affects other areas of your life, you have the connection and inspiration to make it work,» as mentioned by Ellen Ercolini, a career and life coach.

Being A Valued Part of The Team: As suggested by Mary Hladio, founder and president of Ember Carriers Leadership Group, an organizational performance consulting firm.

"Someone who genuinely loves their job is more satisfied and likely more motivated and productive during their time at work. It is unlikely that they will complain or begrudgingly complete tasks at the minimum level of effort, and instead they will be engaged in their work, proactive and, furthermore, interested in motivating co-workers in the mission and goals."

Earning More Money: Doing what you love will have a significant positive impact on your wallet.

Better Health: Author Walter Meyer said, «The tension and pain of doing a job every day that you detest has to take its toll in terms of higher blood pressure, headaches and the rest.»

Added Respect: Executive coach Kathi Elster says "People who love their jobs often spend extra time making sure they are doing their best work, which said will undoubtedly be noticed by supervisors and peers." Going beyond the expected.

Enhanced Home Life: Those who love their work will also have a more enjoyable home life. «Instead of coming home with stress and tension headaches, we return home at night with more energy for ourselves and our families,» as suggested by Melissa Heisler, Personal and business coach.

Improved Productivity: Numerous studies have shown that employees who are involved in their work have a higher productivity rate,» said by Cheryl Palmer, a career coach and professional résumé writer. «Especially since employers are asking more of their employees than before, it helps to love what you do so that you can meet the challenges of the job.»

Stronger Mentally: Viktor Frankl's book, "Man's Search for Meaning," which notes people need a guiding purpose in order to live a happy and health life. "It is important to do something we love for a living because our work lives will then provide meaning and purpose, which are associated with psychological well-being and health," said by expert in organizational culture and a professor in the W. P. Carey School of Business at Arizona State University, Angelo Kinicki.

Serving Other Better: Finance consultant Derek Olsen believes, "The person who loves their job is much more likely to be better at doing the job," Olsen said. "That means more quality goods and better service for the customer."

Dr. Suresh Devnani

Everyone in my school knew that I was going to go to art school and become a fashion designer. That was always the plan. Imagine their surprise when I finally ended up working with my father. Why would I do that? Throughout Middle and High School, all I wanted to be was an artist. When I got to high school and could choose what classes to take, I took every art class that was available. Painting, drawing, photography, you name it—I took the class. I was researching art schools that had specializations in fashion design. I had it all planned out. I even won an award for the most promising artist from my school.

Then I finally decided to join my fathers business. I got to thinking. Wouldn't I make more money if I went into my fathers thriving business instead of being an unknown fashion designer. I loved the energy of doing business and I was good in sales. I could buy whatever I wanted, and I immediately started on the top. Having a nice house, a fancy car. I'm not proud of it, but I bottled up that part of myself and packed it away—the thing I was most passionate about.

Running a successful business of my own until 2000 and then loosing it all, made me realize, how wrong I was taking the short cut to success, leaving my true passion behind.

I started taking online classes where I was able to expand my true passion which was now more inclined towards training and sharing my life's journey in order to help all those who are uncertain and need help in finding their true calling. I am very fortunate to have things work out after all. I am finally doing what I love to do and making money doing it.

Happiness Reinvented

One must realize that is more important that you are happy and get to do what you are passionate about every day and get paid less for it than to dread getting up in the morning because you dislike what you do.

But above all, here's the reality: Life is racing by us, and every second of every day, we are *dying*. That is not something to be afraid about, but it's true. Nobody makes it out of here alive. And in those moments we have, while life may seem infinitely long and infinitely boring to some, we hear others say that it's important to stop once in a while and smell the flowers. But that's the thing, why should I **'smell the flowers?'** This old wise piece of advice is exactly what's causing us to be unhappy. Because if I had to stop and 'smell the flowers' every now and again, that would imply that I didn't live among the flowers. And here's the shocking realization: **Why not?**

You may be saying I can't! 'I have to impress my friends, drive a BMW some day, own a private jet some day, fly down to Bora Bora once a year, and in return for all these luxuries, I am going to spend the majority of my life (from 18 to 60 years old), working a job that I don't like.' **Sound's worth it?** When I ask this, I sometimes get the response, 'YES', 'YES IT DOES SOUND WORTH IT', 'Sam are you kidding me? Of course! Haven't you seen the new Rolls Royce Wraith? I am going to buy that some day'. And so life goes on. And yes, it is great to have a nice big home and drive a nice car, but in the end of the day, **if you did not feel complete without it, you are definitely not going to feel complete with it.** That contentment you imagine does not come from wealth or power, **it comes from doing what you were meant to do; living out your dreams.**

And if you think having a billion dollars is your dream, then maybe it's time to rethink that. Because **that's every ones dream.** Including mine. **But there is a dream unique to you, your inner calling, that when realized, will bring you a much greater euphoria and peace than** you have ever know.

"I think the pursuit of happiness is the pursuit of reality because illusion never leaves us ultimately happy."

— Parker Palmer

5

PURSUIT OF HAPPINESS

Ask anyone these days and they will say that they want to be happier. But does anyone know what will make him or her truly happier?

In most cases, when one says that they are happy they mean they are content with their life and that they are experiencing on regular basis; pleasing emotions, pleasure, joy, enthusiasm and delight and experiencing minimal negative emotions. This kind of happiness is commonly known as normal happiness.

Normal happiness is connected to our daily life; having money in our bank account, having good health, being successful in our current position, having a family, friends or others who show us positive affections. One must understand that normal happiness is conditional and can change due to many uncontrollable things.

Another key setback to normal happiness is that often our focus is based on short-term gains, we eventually pay for this happiness with our failing health, relationships and personal growth; working long hours in pursuit of this happiness, forgetting about our health and dear relationships. The pursuit of normal happiness is based on the belief that happiness exists outside of us.

So what is True Happiness?

After living most of my life in Normal Happiness, I found my true happiness when I started meditating, after a few weeks into mindful meditation, I started to feel a deeper sense of inner well-being, peace and vitality that I have realized exists within all of us. This began to give me an appreciation of the world around me, and how much I used to take it for granted. The people, the things, the sights, the sounds. To experience true happiness, one must feel a deep sense of gratitude for simply being alive.

At times, I know it is hard to accept meditation as being a realistic solution to tackling life, but just like I did, I dare you to give it a try.

True happiness is free from our life situation. Truly happy people have the ability to feel emotions deeply and fully, and are aware and present to their thoughts and emotions without getting entangled in them.

The simple secret is anyone can experience true happiness simply by changing their thoughts, by practicing gratitude,

Happiness Reinvented

being kind and living mindfully. From my personal experience this is important and we all have to play a part.

This point is further confirmed by author and Harvard Researcher, Sonja Lyubomirsky in her book "The How of Happiness" she suggest 12 evidence-based happiness-increasing strategies whose practice is supported by scientific research.[2]

1. Expressing Gratitude
2. Cultivating Optimism
3. Avoiding Overthinking and Social Comparison
4. Practicing Acts of Kindness
5. Nurturing Social Relationships
6. Developing Strategies for Coping
7. Learning to Forgive
8. Increasing Flow Experiences
9. Savoring Life's Joys
10. Committing to Your Goals
11. Practicing Religion and Spirituality
12. Taking Care of Your Body:
    - Meditation
    - Physical Activity
    - Acting Like a Happy Person

For True Happiness we need to fundamentally change our way of being in the world and change the way we live our life.

There are two Approaches to True Happiness

1. On an Everyday level, there are many ways we can train our mind in happiness. For example, we can choose loving thoughts, words, and actions. The more we cultivate love, compassion, joy and impartiality, the more we will become a vibrant source of happiness for others and ourselves.

2. On a Reflective level, when we are connected with our true nature, happiness will arise naturally. Even though negative emotions that arise like sadness, anger, worry, or fear, will be cleared from our mind as we would understand that these being part of our learning process.

These above two approaches are interconnected in cultivating happiness. Actively engaging in positive thoughts, words, and deeds brings us closer to our true nature. When we are in touch with our true nature, these positive qualities spontaneously manifest.

So How Do You Find True Happiness?

These days, so many people are questioning how to find happiness again.

Happiness Reinvented

Yet the path to happiness is a simple one:

Eliminate negative attitudes, actions, and words. Especially those that are foundation to suffering for self and others.

Adopt positive attitudes, actions, and words. Especially those that help in building happiness for self and others.

Reconnect with your true nature – the wellspring of happiness, inner peace, and a better world – through the practice of meditation.

For all of us who are struggling to define our life beyond material goods, Deepak Chopra has found seven interesting ways in finding true happiness.

His new approach in being happy is based on the following new principles:

1. Life has a purpose. When you live up to that purpose, inner happiness develops.

2. Inner happiness can't be taken away.

3. In place of consumerism, you can base everyday happiness on relationships.

4. In place of distractions, you can fill your time with activities that make your heart grow.

5. You can find a place beyond fear that crises and anxiety cannot touch.

6. You can find a place of peace that stress cannot wear out.

7. Wellness will make your body happy. If only individuals choose to look at their lives and make a real effort to follow even a few of these principles, they will start seeing a longer lasting happiness.

We all need to find our purpose, and the more inspiring that purpose, the happier we shall be. What fragments happiness more than anything else is being lonely and empty as one fall into a meaningless life?

We must work on our both our mind and body. A good body is one that makes you happy because it supports your mind being happy.

"The struggle of my life created empathy - I could relate to pain, being abandoned, having people not love me."

— Oprah Winfrey

6

BEING EMPATHETIC

For those who don't have a clue what empathy means, empathy is a selfless act, it enables us to learn more about people and relationships with people - it is a crucial life skill to have as it is beneficial to ourselves, others and overall society.

Empathy is the ability to see the world as another person, to share and understand another person's feelings, needs, concerns and or being in their emotional state.

Being empathetic consists of two components:

- **Effective Communication**
- **Robust Imagination**

Empathy is a skill that can be developed and, as with most interpersonal skills, empathizing (at some level) comes naturally to most people. Most of us can think of examples when we have felt empathy for others or when others have been empathetic towards you. Imagine a colleague being stressed at work due to an ill-fated situation in his/ her personal life; their productivity falls and they miss their deadline. If someone was empathetic they might try to release their work pressures and offer to help them out. They could easily imagine themselves being in the same position and someone coming to their rescue.

Effective Communication

Understanding is the desired outcome or goal in any communication process. Basic understanding is easily achieved but a deeper understanding is the result of effective communication. This involves overcoming the various barriers to communication, being able to express yourself effectively verbally and non-verbally, by active listening and clarification and other interpersonal skills.

Robust Imagination

Everybody sees the world differently, based on their experiences and past conditionings, there up bringing, culture, religion, opinions and beliefs. In order to empathize with another person you need to see the world from their viewpoint and therefore need to use some form of imagination as to what their viewpoint is based on, how they see the world and why they see it differently from you. Many people find it easier to empathize with people who are closer to them and have more shared experiences and views.

Happiness Reinvented

We have all been exposed to news stories of drought and famine in various parts of the world, we can feel sorry for those affected and may be able to help in some way. The news we are receiving via the various forms of media are limited, and very few of us have actually shared similar experiences with the people in question and our thoughts cannot truthfully fill in the gaps of information and enable us to be fully empathies. It is most likely that we are feeling sympathetic versus being empathetic.

Sympathy and Empathy are two of the most common misunderstood words in the English language. There are many individuals who have no clue on the difference between these two words. They are actually two separate words that have some important distinctions that every winner should know.

It is fair to state that both sympathy and empathy are acts of feelings. With sympathy though, you feel for the person. You pity or feel sorry for them but you do not necessarily understand what they are actually feeling. As a result of this you tend to have no choice but feel sympathetic for the person because you do not understand the problem or difficulty that they are currently facing. Empathy on the other hand takes a little more imagination, work, or even similar situations to gain empathy for someone. It is most often referred to as higher order in the overall complexity of the human emotions.

You can describe empathy as sharing a feeling with someone. So do you notice the difference between the two so far? With empathy to an extent you are placing yourself in the persons place, you have a good sense of how they feel, and you also understand their feelings to some degree. Sometimes it may seem impossible for someone to feel empathetic to a person's feelings because of their reactions. These reactions involve their thoughts and feelings towards the issue are going to be unique to each and every individual. The idea of empathy though implies a much more active process than sympathy does.

It is hard for you to empathetic to a person's feelings but it can be easy for you to feel sympathy. It is easy for you to feel sympathy for someone who has lost a loved one, has undergone some certain kind of trauma, or have faced some very difficult times.

The difference between empathy and sympathy is one that's lost on many people. Empathy is just recognizing someone else's emotions. Sympathy is usually a reaction.

Empathy is a key element for leadership development in the Gen Y age, where workers are mobile. Dr Daniel Goleman in a Harvard Business Review article entitled "What Makes a Leader?" isolates three reasons for why empathy is so important: In an increase usage of teams, (which he refers to as "cauldrons of bubbling emotions"), the rapid pace of globalization (with cross cultural communication easily leads to misunderstandings) and the growing need to retain talent. "Leaders with empathy," suggests Dr. Goleman, "do more than sympathize with people around them: they use their knowledge to improve their companies in subtle, but important ways." This does not mean that empathetic leader agrees with everyone's view or tries to please everybody. Rather, he or she "thoughtfully considers employees' feelings – along with other factors – in the process of making intelligent decisions."[3]

Therefore empathy is another component required in the winner's mindset and is well-worth cultivating. This soft, and abstract tool in a leader's arsenal can provide hard, and palpable results.

Where does empathy come from?

According to me it is both a process of thinking and an emotion: One needs to use their ability to reason and understand another person's thoughts, feelings, reactions, concerns, motives. By sincerely making an effort to stop and think for a moment about the other person's perspective in order to begin to understand where they are coming from: And then placing emotional ability to care for that person's concern; Caring does not mean that we would always agree with the person, that we would change our position, but it does mean that we would be in tune with what that person is going through, so that we can respond in a manner that acknowledges their thoughts, feelings or concerns.

Winners use empathy to stimulate trust and build bonds; they are promoters of positive communities for the greater good. For many, empathy does not come naturally; they need to train themselves in developing this capacity.

Here are a few realistic tips one can apply to build on their empathy skills.

Listening:

One way to show empathy is through careful listening. Stop talking and truly listen to the other person.

Understanding A Point of View:

To show empathy for another, it's vital to try to understand the other person's thoughts and opinions. It's not enough to know a person is sad or mad.

Sincerity:

If you listen closely and try to understand the person's point of view, you might know what it is that the person needs to hear.

Showing Self-Control:

Another element of empathy is having self-control. For instance, you might want to grab that last hot-selling TV game off the shelf, but if the other person reaching for it perhaps needs or wants it more, you might allow the other individual to have it.

Follow the "93 percent rule".:

Suggested by Professor Emeritus, Albert Mehrabian of UCLA, when communicating about feelings and attitudes, words – the things we say – account for only 7 percent of the total message that people receive. The other 93 percent of the message that we communicate when we speak is contained in our tone of voice and body language.[4] It is therefore, crucial to spend some time to understand how others persons attitudes and feelings towards us.

Being Fully Present When You Are With People:

Don't check your email, play a game on your mobile or look at your watch or take phone calls when someone is talking to you.

Smile at People:

This one is true magic.

Encourage People:

Especially the quiet ones, when they speak up in meetings. A simple thing like an attentive nod can boost people's confidence. Give genuine recognition and praise.

Give Praise:

Use genuine words which are memorable, like saying that "You are an asset to this team because..."; "This was pure genius"; "I would have missed this if you hadn't picked it up."

Take A Genuine Personal Interest In People:

Show people that you care, and genuine curiosity about their lives. Ask them questions about their hobbies, their challenges, their families, and their aspirations.

Dr. Suresh Devnani

To be winner in anything, one must concentrate on developing their leadership skills.

Winners add value simply by being present with their team members. They inspire and motivate. They have the experience to say the right things to people to help them understand what's needed, and they can influence people to support a cause.

Winners are talented and effective leaders who can lead any organization, to its ultimate success. To be a winner one must acquire these leadership skills on to themselves and their team members.

"Do not ruin today with mourning tomorrow."

— Catherynne M. Valente

7

FEAR OF LOSING LOVED ONES

Concentrate on how they lived, not on how they passed away.

Remember the great moments of life they spent and celebrated with you.

No one has control over death, some of us leave abruptly, and some will suffer through long-term pain before departing. Overall death should not hinder on the circumstances of memorial. Instead we should celebrate life.

Recently I met this wonderful couple that had lost their precious child in a horrific accident, the child was about to graduate from high school and adored by everyone. Till today the parents ask why this happened, and why now?

I felt immediate sympathy for their pain and tried to be empathetic and sense the immense suffering they must be encountering. I also do have a son who will be graduating from High School, if I did loose him, my world will definitely turn upside down. We as parents have so many hopes to see the best for our children that we forget that we are not in control of their lives.

Grief is not an uncommon reaction right after someone's passing and is the normal internal feeling ones experiences in reaction to a loss, while remembrance is the state of having experienced that loss.

Extended sorrow is a reaction to loss that lasts more than a year and the grief reaction influencing all of sufferer's close relationships, upsetting their beliefs, and ensuing in the bereaved experiencing an ongoing longing for their deceased loved one.

Mourning is the outward manifestation of the loss of a loved one and usually involves socially controlled rituals that help make sense of the end of their loved one's life and gives assembly to what can feel like a very puzzling time. It is influenced by personal, familial, cultural, religious, and societal beliefs and customs.

The possible negative effects of a grief reaction can be significant and are often provoked by grief triggers, events that remind the grieving individual of their loved one, or the conditions surrounding their loss.

Individuals who are mourning that feel the death of their loved one is unexpected or violent are at greater risk for suffering from major depression, posttraumatic stress disorder (PTSD), or prolonged grief.

The seven emotional stages of Grief

- Shock or Disbelief
- Denial
- Bargaining
- Guilt
- Anger
- Depression
- Acceptance and Hope

Simple Ways to Help Someone Who's Grieving

Most of us are never prepared to help a family member or a friend or some stranger who is mourning a loss.

Here are some simple, yet thoughtful ways I that I apply:

Listen

Simply make a space, there's no need to rush in with words of comfort, especially if they don't come naturally. Allow the bereaved to express their sorrow with your companionable silence

Never Rush An Emotional Moment

See the moment through, a common impulse when someone gets choked up with grief is to change the subject and try to shift to safer emotional ground. Pause. Offer a hug.

Speak About The Person That Passed Away

Recall or state how the person inspired you or made you happy. Don't avoid mentioning the person who died; he or she is still very much in the minds of grieving family and friends. When they naturally come to mind, don't be afraid to say things like, "Wouldn't Patricia have loved this dress?" or, "I can just hear John saying, 'It's a great day for a run!'

Be Honest Over Clichés

If you're speechless, admit it. There's no "right" thing to say to a survivor, but there are plenty of wrong things never to say to someone who's grieving.

Try, "I don't know what to say. Please know I'm thinking about you." Or, "I can't imagine what each day is like for you now. I'm here for you."

Compassion

Winners must have compassion and be sincere in never allowing living beings to suffer – from any form of physical and or emotional distress –one must have combined sympathetic concern for everything.

Compassion is natural human default; we don't have to force it; we just need to be open to sorrow and strain in the other person; open our heart, and let compassion flow through us.

Mahatma Gandhi achieved independence for India through non-violence. The true expression of non-violence is compassion. Some people seem to think that compassion is just a passive emotional response instead of rational stimulus to action. To feel sincere compassion one must develop a feeling of closeness to others combined with a sense of accountability for their wellbeing. Real compassion develops when we want happiness and not suffering for others, and further we recognize that they have every right to have this.

Compassion induces us to reach out to all living beings, including our so-called adversaries, and those individuals who upset us. Typically our sense of compassion is partial and prejudiced. We offer these feelings only for our family and friends and those who help us. People we see as enemies and whom we are indifferent are barred from our concern. That is not sincere compassion. We must practice compassion on universal basis. Further it must be accompanied by genuine feeling of responsibility.

I would like to end this chapter with the following quote.

Life is eternal, and love is immortal,

and death is only a horizon;

and a horizon is nothing save the limit of our sight.

Rossiter Worthington Raymond

"It is in your moments of decision that your destiny is shaped."

— Tony Robbins

8

DECISION MAKING FOR WINNERS

Throughout history man has made decisions, which have affected every aspect of life. Communally, these decisions have brought us to where we are today: to an environment marked by economics instability, social unpredictability and environmental dilapidation. It is evident that we need Winners, who will make decisions, which are based on the greater good, not only focused on the attainment of a single goal or locating a solution to an immediate problem.

We need leaders who are not afraid to include in their decision making process the wider social, economic and environmental considerations their actions will impact.

Most business schools preach that a decision made by a manager is generally considered 'effective' if it solves a given problem; but in today's environment, decisions often have a variety of other consequences - desired or not - which can deteriorate or enhance the quality of the original decision. In this connected world, we need decision makers who solve problems applying a winners approach.

Winners make decisions by encouraging all stakeholders to be aware of their actions and understand the impact their decisions will have on the whole; they are responsible and accountable for their decisions and inspire everyone to be part of the ongoing process. Following are some ideologies that can help in building the appropriate winning mind frame.

Develop Your View

In order to lead, one must understand the reasons for their actions. As the Dalai Lama suggests, "The nature of our motivation determines the character of our work." In the business sense, this means thinking analytically about the consequences of any overarching objectives as well as the purpose behind daily procedures. It also means remaining aware of not only your own interests but the interests of all those you lead.

Establish The Right Conduct

Winners ensure that they have the best intentions applied towards all that they practice.

Train Your Mind

As the Dalai Lama explains that the untrained mind is like a monkey jumping around in a tree, excited, and unable to concentrate. Further the Dalai Lama suggests that "The leader has to recognize when negative emotions like frustration, impatience, anger, lack of self-confidence, jealousy, greed start to influence his thought processes," "These negative thoughts and emotions not only can lead to wrong decisions but also waste mind energy." Through easy to apply mindfulness or meditation techniques one can control their emotions.

Focus On Happiness

By asking two simple questions, a winner can discover how best to motivate those surrounding them. What makes you happy? What makes you unhappy? According to the Dalai Lama, happiness is the highest universal form of motivation.

Stay Interconnected

Interconnect—the idea that people only truly exist in relation with other people. The interconnected leader sees themselves as the producers of propulsions in an interconnected system to fulfill the purpose. When one desires—anything from another individual, it activates an idea and sets off a chain reaction for creative productivity. It is a winner's task to achieve and bolster impulses among all stakeholders, and even opponents.

Stay Positive

Its no secret being in charge is hard and in some cases a lonely proposition. But, instead, the Dalai Lama encourages a more optimistic approach to life. "Appreciate how rare and full of potential your situation is in this world, then take joy in it, and use it to your best advantage," every problem has a solution, and having the right attitude from the beginning may help you find it.

"Our greatness lies not so much in being able to remake the world as being able to remake ourselves."

— Mahatma Gandhi

From my experience and through the various research papers I have written, there is one quality that all winners posses that is self-awareness. The best thing leaders can is to improve their effectiveness in becoming more aware of what motivates them and their decision-making. They have a clear perception of their personal strengths and weaknesses; they know what motivates them; they know what they truly value; and they are aware of their potential and even their thoughts. It is self-awareness that allows the Winners to be true Leaders. Winners need to be able to project conviction while concurrently remaining modest to new ideas and opposing opinions.

Without self-awareness, one is not truly connected to their feelings, feelings that can later cause struggles and disagreements in one life. Self-awareness includes understanding ourselves. No one is perfect and a deep understanding of ourselves, our fears, and the things that excite us can all help us to live in the greater world and in harmony and peace with others. Self-awareness also includes the basics such as being clear about what we like to do and what we don't like. It can include feelings about events and how they impact and change us. Self-awareness can just be understanding and feeling comfortable with one's self-behavior.

"You teach best what you need to learn."

— Richard Bach

9

OUR ATTITUDE REFLECTS OUR LIFE

The more I think about this, I realize the above statement by Richard Bach to be true. I do teach what I need to learn. I would definitely say that there are numerous issues in my life that I need help with and one way to help myself is by teaching and then learning in return through individuals who interact with me. This analytical feedback then helps me in return in remodeling my workshops.

Whatever we sincerely believe about ourselves is reflected in our daily lives. If we think negatively, then our attitude will be one full of pessimism for almost everything. If we have a foundation of positive attitude, we will definitely receive all the RICHES we desire.

"There is a basic law that like attracts like. Negative thinking definitely attracts negative results."

Dr. Suresh Devnani

— Norman Vincent Peale

One needs to live their life full of Passion and Purpose, always be positive, believe in themselves, pursue their dreams, and always want to be healthy. A positive attitude can change your life forever.

Positivity is achieved when we have the ability to see things in their real state. The skill of "seeing" is a deep comprehension of the real truth of knowing the purpose of our being.

Our attitude brings responses both inwardly and outwardly. The outer responses are responses advocated to us by others that can be either positive or negative. The inner responses are emerging from our conscious mind through our subconscious mind that can be either positive or negative, depending on our self-awareness.

One must recognize that with a negative attitude we will harm ourselves psychologically, psychically and metaphysically from all the damaging conditions that are a direct result of our current attitude.

By having a negative attitude we destroy ourselves psychologically as our failure thoughts become part of our subconscious mind affecting our daily life, and day-by-day we see a multiplication of our difficulties and failures.

By having a negative attitude we destroy ourselves psychically as our negative thoughts are emitted, asking for a multiplication of our difficulties and failures.

Happiness Reinvented

It is no hidden secret that our positive attitude can destroy all the above negativity and build ourselves in achieving our success through our psychologically, psychically and metaphysically.

Winners have a positive attitude, which is a prerequisite to your success. You can be as positive as you want to be if you will simply think about the future, focus on the solution and look for the good. If you do what other successful people do, if you use your mind to exert mental control over the situation, you will be positive and cheerful most of the time. And you will reap the benefits enjoyed by all successful people.

Winners empower and motivate their family, friends, employees, customers, suppliers, bankers; one simply needs to be a sincere, positive and cheerful person. Be the kind of person who never uses discouraging words. Be easygoing, welcoming, friendly, patient, tolerant and open-minded. Make people feel comfortable being around you.

Positive thinking is the key to good health, happiness, and overall wellbeing. The more positive you lead your life, the better and happier your life will be in every area of your life.

With practice, one can begin to learn the means that can help one in achieving true happiness.

Over time, I have come to identify some rules that have helped me reach my goals quicker.

Dr. Suresh Devnani

The Blueprint to Positive Personal Development

- Be caring towards everyone you meet
- Pardon all those who try to harm you
- Remember that you turn out to be what you think
- Find new novel ways to help those who are not as fortunate as you
- Continuously pursue knowledge and truth
- Always be truthful
- Appreciate for all that you have
- Never give up

After identifying these principles, I needed a way to make them a part of my life. So I studied some more. What I found is that the best way to make something a part of your life is to set a goal and follow through on it.

One of the most significant step one must take towards achieving there greatest potential in life is learning the skill required in monitoring there attitude and how it influences there work performance, relationships and everyone that surrounds them.

I have always enjoyed asking the following essential question from those who attend my seminars, workshops, or even my family and friends: What kind of attitude are

Happiness Reinvented

you in? Commonly I receive puzzled looks. In reality, most individuals are not aware of the attitude they are in. Most know when they are thirsty or they have headache, but a majority of us don't have a good handle on our attitude. Attitude is everything, it oversees the way one observes the world and the way the world observes us.

As individuals we all have a choice. We can adopt our inner dialogue that provides self-encouragement and self-motivation, or we can select the one that pushes towards self-defeat and self-pity. Life is full of challenges, however we must tackle these challenges with a positive attitude.

We all go through difficult situations in life. The key is to realize it's not what happens to you that matter; it's how you choose to respond.

Our mind is a programmed computer, we choose the software we want to maintain or delete. Our inner voice is the software that programs our attitude that regulates the way we present our self to those surrounding us. We ultimately have the control over this programming. We must understand that whatever we input into this computer and finally reflected in the out put.

The noisiest and most dominant voice one hears is commonly known, as inner voice is also one of the harshest self-critics. It can help or push you to fail, depending on the messages one allows. It can be positive or negative.

Side effects of this inner voice include low self-esteem, stress, fear, bitterness, rage and failure to handle change. It requires serious effort for one to scrutinize the roots of a damaging attitude, but the rewards of freeing ourselves from this unnecessary baggage can last for a lifetime.

Following are some techniques that I apply regularly in order to improve my attitude:

Affirmations – are made up of words charged with power, conviction and faith. You send a positive response to your subconscious, which accepts whatever you tell it. When repeated several times each day, every day, serve to reprogram your subconscious with positive thinking. A few have been shared in various chapters to help you in various avenues.

Self-Motivation - what inspires you to take action to change your life. Self-motivation requires enthusiasm, a positive outlook, and a positive physiology.

Visualization - Visualization works well to improve attitude. Various studies done on the best athletes, surgeons, engineers and artists use affirmations and visualizations either consciously or subconsciously to enhance and focus their skills.

Positive Attitude Internal Dialogue - Our little voice that we listen to all day long acts like a seed in that it programs our brain and affects our behavior. When we supersede our past negative programming by erasing or replacing it with a conscious, positive internal voice that will help us see positive direction.

Watch over our Words - our words cannot be taken back

once we have released them to the universe. What we speak initiates what is already in our hearts based upon all the things we have come to believe about ourselves. We have the ability to produce a direct path to success by simply saying the right words.

Positive Greeting – Always greet and give a positive respond by saying life is beautiful, and I am enjoying day after day. Our life itself is a beautiful gift.

Staying Motivated – Enthusiasm empowers us to take action, which allows us to place our commitment, determination and spirit into action.

Humor - is a powerful motivator. Living in humor allows our stress to convert into positive energy, which in order places our positive attitude into action. Besides this there are multiple health benefits.

For most of us, taking in new knowledge and learning new skills is an ongoing part of life. Now we see that a truly successful life requires that we pay special attention to the areas that can have the greatest positive impact on our quality of life and degree of overall success.

Attitude is one of the most important elements for bringing together "who you are" with "what you do." It may not be everything, but it's important enough that nothing else compares to it. Once you see firsthand how changing your attitude changes your reality, your life will be forever transformed.

"Health is the greatest possession. Contentment is the greatest treasure. Confidence is the greatest friend. Non-being is the greatest joy."

— Lao Tzu

10

AWAKENING AND LOVING YOUR TRUE SELF

Why are so many people confused about whom they really are and what is their true personal identity? While it may seem like you should robotically know how to be yourself, in reality that is seldom the case.

When we think about it, so many things in life depend on our aptitude to connect with our true self. After all, how are we supposed to know what we should be doing or whom we should be doing it with if we don't even know who we truly are?

The expectations set by those around us strongly influence our identity. Many of these choices we think we have made in life were most likely programmed into us by the expectations of those whose approval we desired. It is amazing to what level people will adapt to gain the endorsement of others.

Then there are the expectations that we put on ourselves because we think we have to. This could include anything from us receiving straight A's at school, to the employment we would walk away from if it were not due to the high salary we were receiving.

One must establish a relationship with their true inner being, to achieve inner peace and balance this can only be gained when we connect with the love that lies within us. We all are filled with self-love and have the ability to attain any form of happiness and or joy we desire.

We must learn to recognize ourselves by sitting back and truly listening to our hearts and bodies, taking risks and allowing ourselves the room to do so. How can one hear what their inner self is trying so frantically to say if all we do is sprint from one task to another to societal engagements to networking events and never taking the time in appraising what is really important?

Are You Truly Happy Being So Engaged?

Are you actually growing into the person that you want to spend the rest of your life being?

There is no time line or stop watch telling us when we should start this journey of self-discovery. There is no wrong time. There is only the right time – any age, any situation.

Happiness Reinvented

Truly knowing yourself is the first step in realizing a more conscious, unpretentious lifestyle.

Love is the answer to our entire being. Love is Consciousness. Love is bliss. It does not exist for the sake of someone else. It is absolutely free. One must walk on this inner path of love, realize love, and merge into the infinite of love.

If one wants to experience love, they need to start loving themself. First they must love their own body, then everything that is connected to the body, and then master all the functions of body, the inner Self, which will allow one to be finally liberated.

It is remarkable that we keep looking for love, even though we are all born of love. We come out of love. All of us are nothing but vibrations of love. We are sustained by love, and in the end we merge back into love…. This world is nothing but a school of love; our relationships with our spouses, with our children, parents, relatives and friends are part of the learning process from which we are suppose to learn about true love and devotion.

Yet the love we experience through others is just a hint of the love of the inner Self. There is an inspiring place within us where love resides. The love that beats in the cavity of the heart does not depend on anything outside. It does not expect anything. It is completely impartial.

It is critical that we learn how to love our self. Self-love is the key ingredient that leads to wellbeing, joy, self-empowerment, and our ability to create and enjoy the kind of life we want. One will not enjoy happiness if they are not at peace with themselves. Our relationship with our self is the fundamental to our being.

From the mystical standpoint, when our attention centered on inward to our self then we are able to experience our connection with Life, with God, with truth of being.

From the human viewpoint, every relationship we ever have with someone else accurately mirrors one or more aspects of the relationship that we have with our self.

With over 5 million hits per month on Google, the phrase "find myself", reveals one clear thing that so many of us feel disconnected from our true self and want to reconnect to our true calling.

Following are some components that can help in connecting with your true self.

Internal Alignment

Being truthful is a key ingredient to internal harmony. To be yourself means that you need to identify your core standards and align with them.

Recognize Your Personal Values

To truly be yourself, it is vital that you identify those values and make every effort to live by them.

Choose Your Passions Carefully

You might think that you have very little control over your

passions, but nothing could be further from the truth. To make sure that our passions align with our true self they need to be in harmony with our values and standards. Passions are easily influenced by what we think about and what we take in through our five senses.

Adjust Your Response Patterns

How we respond to the many situations and circumstances in our lives will determine how the world around us responds to us. Most people just react to external stimuli. How much more appropriate it is to respond in a way that supports our values and reinforces our sense of self-honesty. If someone pushes your buttons and you just react, then they were the ones controlling you. To be yourself you need to consciously choose your response.

Cultivate Positive Beliefs About Yourself

Being yourself is very difficult if you believe that you are worthless or undeserving, which of course isn't true. Make it a habit to cultivate positive feelings about yourself as a person. Commend yourself for all the wonderful ways you contribute to the world around you. If you give yourself the approval you deserve then your identity won't depend on approval from outside sources.

"Happiness doesn't depend on any external conditions, it is governed by our mental attitude."

— Dale Carnegie

EPILOGUE

Ultimately, we all aim to be happy. Most of us are confused about what is happiness and spend all our life trying to find happiness that we are unable to define. The irony is that we allow chances of feeling happy to be lost in our struggle for mediocre survival. It is a given right for you to be happy to succeed and progress in life.

We choose our own actions, beliefs, thoughts and goals that are key elements that lead towards our happiness. Therefore, you and only you can create the perfect blueprint of your happiness by following the method that has worked for many thousands and me.

Your happiness must be an integral part of your life as you hold the key to your emotions and feelings. Do not hold others or their actions responsible for causing you to be unhappy. Select your path through the hurdles of life to arrive upon the happiness you and others deserve.

We must love unconditionally to enjoy unconditional happiness. The feeling of loving someone is to accept the person unconditionally without placing any significance on existing or lacking characteristics. Unconditional love wears away all the negativity and helps in aiding one towards the positive direction allowing all towards happiness, which is unilateral.

Our health, forgiveness, self-acceptance, and empathy supports in building towards our unconditional love and subsequent happiness.

Working towards good health for all is a predating element of happiness. We must take great care of our health. Loving is forgiving. Accepting others as they are and viewing confounds, as a part of enlightenment process is a huge leap towards happiness.

Our personal growth eventually offers enhanced value in our ultimate quest for happiness. One then can allocate importance to numerous values of enhanced life like humility, virtuousness, self-adequacy, individuality, impartiality, and others in the same context.

Where Do You Go From Here?

"Talk is Cheap." I hope you enjoyed reading this book, but crucially, I hope you will use the concepts and techniques to enhance your life. From my experience, however reading is just a start, but if one wants to succeed, actions will count more than words.

One must apply this new knowledge to discover their deepest personal values and passions. These two aspects of your true self define the person that you truly want to be. If you structure your self-expression around these core elements, you will create a deep sense of internal harmony and find the happiness that is ever lasting and contagious.

Unfortunately, in this mad race for survival we miss out simple situations and incidents that could provide us happiness. Family, society, friendship and the government can improve the general atmosphere for the people so that situations causing unhappiness can be reduced. While sustained happiness may not be so much in our hands, no one can deny us moments of pleasure in solitude, in the company of children, while listening to music and so on. The book tries to encourage you to discover such moments yourself.

Now you have the tools…

GO FOR IT!

Notes

1. Sports Visualizations. (n.d.). Llewellyn Worldwide. Retrieved November 20, 2013, from http://www.llewellyn.com/encyclopedia/article/244

2. Lyubomirsky, Sonja. The How of Happiness: A Scientific Approach to Getting the Life You Want. New York: Penguin, 2008. Print.

3. "January 2004." What Makes a Leader? N.p., n.d. Web. 21 Nov. 2013.

4. "What's Empathy Got to Do With It?" Empathy and Leadership. N.p., n.d. Web. 21 Nov. 2013.

www.ingramcontent.com/pod-product-compliance
Lightning Source LLC
Chambersburg PA
CBHW070513090426
42735CB00012B/2766